Phuket Travel Guide 2023

Unlocking Phuket: Your Insider's Guide to Thailand's Tropical Paradise

Agatha Josiane

Copyright © 2023 by Agatha Josiane

All rights reserved. No part of this publication may be reproduced, distributed, or transmitted in any form or by any means, including photocopying, recording, or other electronic or mechanical methods, without the prior written permission of the publisher, except in the case of brief quotations embodied in critical reviews and certain other noncommercial uses permitted by copyright law.

Table of Content

Chapter 1: Introduction to Phuket
A Serendipitous Journey: Uniting Hearts in Phuket
1.1 About Phuket
1.2 History of Phuket
1.3 Geographical Overview
1.4 Climate and Weather
1.5 Cultural Background

Chapter 2: Planning Your Trip
2.1 Best Time to Visit Phuket
2.2 Duration of Stay
2.3 Budgeting and Expenses
2.4 Visa and Entry Requirements
2.5 Packing Essentials

Chapter 3: Getting to Phuket
3.1 By Air
3.2 By Sea
3.3 By Road

Chapter 4: Accommodation Options
4.1 Luxury Resorts and Hotels

4.2 Budget-Friendly Accommodations
4.3 Boutique and Unique Stays
4.4 Beachfront Villas
4.5 Homestays and Guesthouses

Chapter 5: Exploring Phuket's Beaches
5.1 Patong Beach
5.2 Kata Beach
5.3 Karon Beach
5.4 Surin Beach
5.5 Nai Harn Beach

Chapter 6: Phuket's Cultural and Historical Sites
6.1 Old Phuket Town
6.2 Big Buddha
6.3 Wat Chalong
6.4 Phuket Old Town Weekend Market
6.5 Phang Nga Bay

Chapter 7: Outdoor Activities and Adventures
7.1 Snorkeling and Diving
7.2 Island Hopping
7.3 Elephant Sanctuaries
7.4 Jungle Trekking
7.5 Zip-lining and Canopy Tours

Chapter 8: Phuket's Nightlife and Entertainment
8.1 Bangla Road
8.2 Night Markets
8.3 Cabaret Shows
8.4 Beach Clubs and Bars
8.5 Muay Thai Boxing Matches

Chapter 9: Shopping in Phuket
9.1 Central Festival Phuket
9.2 Jungceylon Shopping Mall
9.3 Phuket Weekend Market
9.4 Local Handicrafts and Souvenirs
9.5 Floating Markets

Chapter 10: Phuket's Gastronomy
10.1 Traditional Thai Cuisine
10.2 Seafood Delights
10.3 Local Street Food
10.4 International Dining Options
10.5 Cooking Classes and Food Tours

Chapter 11: Spa and Wellness in Phuket
11.1 Traditional Thai Massage
11.2 Luxury Spa Retreats

11.3 Yoga and Meditation Centers
11.4 Detox and Wellness Programs
11.5 Healing and Alternative Therapies

Chapter 12: Family-Friendly Activities
12.1 Phuket Aquarium
12.2 Phuket Trickeye Museum
12.3 Splash Jungle Water Park
12.4 Phuket Elephant Sanctuary
12.5 Phuket Butterfly Garden and Insect World

Chapter 13: Day Trips from Phuket
13.1 Phi Phi Islands
13.2 Similan Islands
13.3 Phang Nga Bay
13.4 James Bond Island
13.5 Krabi and Ao Nang

Chapter 14: Sustainable Tourism in Phuket
14.1 Ecotourism Initiatives
14.2 Responsible Diving and Snorkeling
14.3 Community-Based Tourism Projects
14.4 Wildlife Conservation Efforts
14.5 Supporting Local Businesses

Chapter 15: Phuket's Festivals and Events

15.1 Songkran (Thai New Year)
15.2 Vegetarian Festival
15.3 Loy Krathong
15.4 Phuket Old Town Festival
15.5 Phuket International Blues Rock Festival

Chapter 16: Transportation in Phuket
16.1 Tuk-Tuks and Taxis
16.2 Motorbike Rentals
16.3 Songthaews (Shared Minibuses)
16.4 Grab and Uber Services
16.5 Public Bus System

Chapter 17: Safety Tips and Travel Advice
17.1 Health and Medical Services
17.2 Scam Awareness
17.3 Beach Safety
17.4 Respect for Local Customs
17.5 Emergency Contacts

Chapter 18: Learning Basic Thai Phrases
18.1 Greetings and Common Expressions
18.2 Ordering Food and Drinks
18.3 Asking for Directions
18.4 Shopping and Bargaining
18.5 Emergency Phrases

Chapter 19: Beyond Phuket: Exploring the Region
19.1 Krabi Province
19.2 Phang Nga Province
19.3 Phi Phi Islands
19.4 Khao Lak
19.5 Phuket's Nearby Islands

Chapter 20: Conclusion and Farewell to Phuket
20.1 Reflections on Your Phuket Journey
20.2 Memories and Souvenirs
20.3 Planning Your Next Visit
20.4 Saying Goodbye to Phuket
20.5 Acknowledgments and Credits

Chapter 1: Introduction to Phuket

A Serendipitous Journey: Uniting Hearts in Phuket

Amidst the bustling crowd of first-time travelers, a diverse group of individuals found themselves embarking on a journey to the captivating island of Phuket. Each person brought their unique perspectives, dreams, and aspirations, unaware of the profound impact this adventure would have on their lives.

Midé, a young woman from Nigeria, had always yearned to explore the world beyond her familiar surroundings. Phuket, with its exotic allure, was the perfect destination to satiate her wanderlust. Nervous yet filled with anticipation, she joined the group, eager to immerse herself in the wonders that lay ahead.

As the days unfolded, the group embarked on thrilling adventures, bonding over snorkeling escapades amidst vibrant coral reefs and exploring hidden trails that led to breathtaking waterfalls. They reveled in the beauty of Phuket's picturesque landscapes, from the majestic limestone cliffs to the lush tropical jungles, capturing moments of awe and wonder.

In the heart of Phuket's bustling streets, Midé found herself enthralled by the rich tapestry of Thai culture. She marveled at the ornate temples, adorned with intricate details and vibrant colors, and eagerly participated in the local festivals, immersing herself in the joyous celebrations that enveloped the island.

It was during an evening stroll along the serene shores of Patong Beach that Midé encountered Aiden, a fellow traveler from Ireland, who shared her passion for adventure and an insatiable curiosity for the unknown. Their chance of meeting blossomed into a deep friendship as they explored Phuket together, indulging in the tantalizing flavors of Thai cuisine, getting lost in the labyrinthine streets of Phuket Town, and sharing stories and laughter late into the night.

Alongside their newfound friends, Midé and Aiden discovered the power of connection and the beauty of embracing diversity. They forged bonds that transcended cultural barriers, finding comfort and support in the shared experiences of their fellow travelers. The group became a family, united by their collective desire to embrace Phuket's treasures and create lasting memories.

As the sun began to set on their Phuket adventure, Midé couldn't help but reflect on the transformative power of travel. She had grown in ways she never imagined, embracing the vibrant spirit of Phuket and cherishing the lifelong friendships she had made along the way. This journey opened her eyes to the beauty of the world and ignited a passion within her to continue exploring, connecting, and discovering the wonders that awaited her beyond the shores of Phuket.

Amid farewells and heartfelt goodbyes, Midé and her fellow travelers departed from Phuket, carrying with them a newfound sense of self, cherished memories, and a shared belief in the transformative power of travel. The island had left an indelible mark on their hearts, a testament to the serendipitous connections and life-changing experiences that can be found in the most unexpected places.

As they scattered to different corners of the globe, Midé and her newfound friends knew that their paths would inevitably diverge, but the memories forged in Phuket would forever bind them together. And perhaps one day, their paths would cross again, reigniting the flames of friendship and wanderlust that had been ignited on that serendipitous journey in Phuket.

1.1 About Phuket

Phuket, the largest island in Thailand, is a tropical paradise nestled in the Andaman Sea. Known for its stunning beaches, vibrant nightlife, and rich cultural heritage, Phuket has become one of the most popular tourist destinations in Southeast Asia. The island offers a diverse range of attractions and activities, catering to the interests of every traveler. Whether you seek relaxation on pristine shores, exhilarating water sports, or a glimpse into the local culture, Phuket promises an unforgettable experience.

1.2 History of Phuket

Phuket's history is a captivating tapestry woven with influences from various civilizations. Originally inhabited by sea gypsies and Malay fishermen, the island later attracted traders from China, India, and Europe. Over the centuries, Phuket became a significant trading port and played a crucial role in maritime trade routes between China and India. The island's name, derived from the Malay word "Bukit," meaning hill, reflects its hilly terrain.

During the 18th century, Phuket became part of the Kingdom of Thailand (formerly known as Siam), and its importance continued to grow. The island thrived due to its tin mining industry and the cultivation of rubber and palm oil plantations. Today, remnants of Phuket's historical past can be seen in its charming old town, ornate temples, and Chinese-style mansions.

1.3 Geographical Overview

Phuket is situated in the Andaman Sea, off the western coast of Thailand's southern region. The island spans an area of approximately 576 square kilometers (222 square miles) and is connected to the mainland by the Sarasin Bridge. Its coastline is adorned with picturesque beaches and stunning limestone cliffs, while the interior is characterized by lush hills and tropical rainforests.

Phuket is part of the larger Phuket Province, which includes 32 smaller islands. The most notable among these islands are Phi Phi Islands, known for their breathtaking beauty and crystal-clear waters. Phuket's strategic location makes it an ideal base for exploring the nearby stunning archipelagos and marine national parks.

1.4 Climate and Weather

Phuket enjoys a tropical monsoon climate, making it a year-round destination with warm temperatures and abundant sunshine. The island experiences two distinct seasons: the dry season (November to April) and the wet season (May to October).

During the dry season, Phuket boasts clear skies, lower humidity levels, and pleasant temperatures ranging from 25 to 32 degrees Celsius (77 to 90 degrees Fahrenheit). This period is ideal for beach activities, water sports, and exploring the island's outdoor attractions.

The wet season brings occasional rain showers and higher humidity. However, it is important to note that rainfall is typically short-lived, and sunny intervals are common even during this time. The wet season offers its charm, with lush green landscapes and fewer crowds. It is worth considering that some water-based activities may be affected by weather conditions during this period.

1.5 Cultural Background

Phuket's cultural heritage is a vibrant blend of Thai, Chinese, and Malay influences. The majority of the population practices Theravada Buddhism, and visitors will find numerous ornate Buddhist temples (wats) scattered across the island. These temples serve as serene sanctuaries and showcase intricate architectural designs and spiritual traditions.

Chinese culture holds a significant presence in Phuket, evident in the elaborate shrines and the annual Phuket Vegetarian Festival. The festival, celebrated by the Chinese community, features colorful processions, impressive firewalking rituals, and displays of devotion and self-mortification.

The island's cultural diversity is further reflected in its cuisine, which offers a tantalizing fusion of Thai and Chinese flavors. Phuket's culinary scene is renowned for its fresh seafood, spicy curries, and unique street food delicacies.

Phuket's rich cultural tapestry is also evident in its vibrant festivals, lively markets, and traditional arts and crafts. Exploring the island provides ample opportunities to immerse oneself in its cultural heritage and engage with the warm and welcoming locals.

Chapter 1 provides a comprehensive introduction to Phuket, encompassing its geographical features, historical significance, climate, and cultural mosaic that shapes the island's identity. Understanding these aspects sets the stage for a deeper exploration of Phuket's wonders and enhances the appreciation of its beauty and diversity.

Chapter 2: Planning Your Trip

2.1 Best Time to Visit Phuket

Choosing the right time to visit Phuket can greatly enhance your travel experience. Phuket enjoys a tropical climate throughout the year, but it does have distinct seasons that can affect your activities and overall enjoyment. The best time to visit Phuket is generally during the dry season, which spans from November to April. This period offers pleasant weather with lower humidity levels and minimal rainfall, making it ideal for beach activities, island hopping, and exploring outdoor attractions.

However, it's important to note that the peak tourist season in Phuket coincides with this dry season, particularly during December and January. This means that popular tourist spots can get crowded, and accommodation and flight prices tend to be higher. If you prefer a quieter and more budget-friendly experience, consider visiting during the shoulder seasons of November or April. These months offer favorable weather conditions while avoiding the peak crowds.

On the other hand, the monsoon season in Phuket occurs from May to October, characterized by higher chances of rainfall and occasional storms. While the number of tourists decreases during this period, some visitors find it appealing as the landscapes become lush and vibrant, and hotel rates are generally lower. However, it's important to be aware of potential disruptions to outdoor activities and boat trips due to rough seas and inclement weather.

2.2 Duration of Stay

The ideal duration of your stay in Phuket depends on your preferences and the activities you wish to pursue. For a comprehensive experience of the island's attractions and to enjoy a relaxed pace, it is recommended to spend at least five to seven days in Phuket. This allows ample time to explore the beautiful beaches, indulge in water sports, visit cultural and historical sites, embark on day trips to nearby islands, and savor the local cuisine.

However, if you have limited time, a shorter stay of three to four days can still provide a taste of Phuket's highlights. In this case, it's advisable to prioritize your must-see attractions and plan your itinerary accordingly. Keep in mind that Phuket offers a diverse range of activities and experiences, so the longer your stay, the more you can immerse yourself in the island's offerings.

2.3 Budgeting and Expenses

When planning your trip to Phuket, it's important to consider your budget and estimate your expenses accurately. Phuket caters to a wide range of budgets, offering options for both luxury travelers and those on a tighter budget.

Accommodation prices vary depending on the location, season, and type of lodging you choose. Luxury resorts and beachfront hotels tend to be more expensive, while guesthouses, hostels, and budget-friendly accommodations offer more affordable options. It's advisable to book accommodation in advance, especially during peak season, to secure the best rates.

In terms of daily expenses, food, and transportation are relatively affordable in Phuket. You can find a wide range of dining options, from street food stalls to high-end restaurants. Sampling local street food is not only delicious but also budget-friendly. Public transportation options, such as local buses and shared minibusses (songthaews), offer inexpensive ways to get around the island. Taxis and tuk-tuks are available but can be more costly, so it's recommended to negotiate fares or use ride-hailing services like Grab.

Additionally, budgeting for activities and excursions is essential. Many popular attractions in Phuket have admission fees or require booking guided tours. It's a good idea to research and prioritize the activities that interest you the most and allocate a portion of your budget accordingly.

2.4 Visa and Entry Requirements

Before traveling to Phuket, it's crucial to understand the visa and entry requirements to ensure a smooth and hassle-free trip. Here is an overview of the visa regulations for most tourists visiting Phuket:

Citizens of many countries are granted visa-free entry for a limited period upon arrival at Phuket International Airport. These visa-exempt countries typically include the United States, Canada, the United Kingdom, Australia, and most European nations. Visitors from these countries are generally allowed to stay for up to 30 days.

If you plan to stay longer than the visa-free period or if your country is not eligible for visa-free entry, you may need to apply for a tourist visa in advance from a Thai embassy or consulate. Tourist visas usually grant a stay of up to 60 days and can be extended once for an additional 30 days while in Thailand.

It's important to check the specific visa requirements for your country of residence before traveling to Phuket, as regulations can vary. The Royal Thai Embassy or Consulate in your home country will provide the most accurate and up-to-date information regarding visa application procedures, required documents, and fees.

It's worth noting that your passport must be valid for at least six months beyond your intended departure date from Thailand. Ensure that you have sufficient blank pages in your passport for immigration stamps.

2.5 Packing Essentials

When packing for your trip to Phuket, it's important to consider the climate, activities, and cultural norms of the destination. Here are some essential items to pack for your Phuket adventure:

Lightweight and breathable clothing: Pack light, loose-fitting clothes made from breathable fabrics such as cotton or linen to stay comfortable in the tropical climate. Don't forget to include swimwear, as you'll likely spend time at the beach or by the pool.

Sun protection: The sun in Phuket can be intense, so pack sunscreen with a high SPF, a wide-brimmed hat, sunglasses, and a lightweight scarf or cover-up for extra protection. A travel-sized umbrella or rain poncho can come in handy during the rainy season.

Insect repellent: Phuket is home to mosquitoes and other insects, especially in wooded or rural areas. Pack insect repellent containing DEET or other effective ingredients to protect yourself from mosquito-borne illnesses.

Comfortable footwear: Bring comfortable walking shoes for exploring attractions and flip-flops or sandals for the beach. If you plan to hike or engage in outdoor activities, consider packing sturdy hiking shoes or water shoes.

Travel adapter and electronics: Thailand uses Type A, B, C, and O electrical outlets. Bring a travel adapter if your devices have different plug types. Don't forget to pack chargers for your electronics, such as smartphones, cameras, and laptops.

Medications and toiletries: Pack any necessary prescription medications and a basic first-aid kit. It's also recommended to bring insect bite cream, diarrhea medication, and any personal toiletries you may need.

Travel documents: Carry a copy of your passport, visa (if required), travel insurance, and any other important travel documents. It's also advisable to have electronic copies stored securely online or in your email for easy access.

By considering these essentials and tailoring your packing list to your specific needs, you can ensure a comfortable and enjoyable trip to Phuket.

Chapter 3: Getting to Phuket

Phuket, an enchanting tropical paradise located in southern Thailand, offers various transportation options for travelers to reach its shores. In this chapter, we explore the different ways to get to Phuket, ensuring a convenient and seamless journey to this captivating island destination.

3.1 By Air

Flying to Phuket is the most common and convenient option for travelers coming from both domestic and international locations. Phuket International Airport (HKT) is well-connected to major cities worldwide, making it easily accessible for visitors from all corners of the globe. Several renowned airlines operate regular flights to and from Phuket, ensuring a wide range of options to suit different travel preferences and budgets.

Upon arrival at Phuket International Airport, travelers can take advantage of various transportation services, such as taxis, private transfers, or car rentals, to reach their accommodations. The airport is located approximately 32 kilometers from Phuket's popular tourist areas, and the journey typically takes around 45 minutes to an hour, depending on traffic conditions.

3.2 By Sea

For those seeking a unique and picturesque journey, arriving in Phuket by sea is an excellent choice. The island is a prominent port of call for many cruise liners and yachts sailing through the Andaman Sea. Phuket's deep-water harbor, Ao Makham, can accommodate large vessels, offering a gateway for maritime travelers to explore the island's treasures.

Cruise liners often include Phuket as part of their itineraries, providing an opportunity to experience the island's beauty while enjoying the amenities and services offered onboard. Private yachts and sailing enthusiasts can also find marinas and anchorages in Phuket, allowing them to enjoy the island at their own pace.

3.3 By Road

Traveling to Phuket by road offers a scenic and adventurous option for those exploring the surrounding regions or arriving from neighboring areas of Thailand. The island is connected to the mainland by the Sarasin Bridge, which spans across the narrow strait between Phuket and Phang Nga provinces.

From major cities in Thailand, such as Bangkok or Chiang Mai, travelers can embark on an exhilarating road trip to Phuket. The journey by car or bus allows for picturesque views of the countryside and the opportunity to visit attractions along the way. Several bus companies operate direct routes to Phuket from various cities, providing an affordable and convenient transportation option.

Additionally, for travelers already in the south of Thailand, there are domestic bus services that connect Phuket to destinations such as

Krabi, Surat Thani (gateway to Koh Samui), and Hat Yai.

It's important to note that while road travel offers an adventurous experience, it is essential to be mindful of local traffic regulations and ensure a safe and comfortable journey.

Conclusion

Getting to Phuket is an exciting part of your travel adventure, with different options available to suit your preferences and travel plans. Whether you choose to fly, sail, or embark on a road trip, each mode of transportation provides its unique charm and allows you to witness the natural beauty of the region. Regardless of how you arrive, Phuket awaits with its pristine beaches, vibrant culture, and warm hospitality, ready to offer you an unforgettable experience.

Chapter 4: Accommodation Options

When it comes to planning your stay in Phuket, you'll find a wide range of accommodation options to suit every budget and preference. From luxurious resorts and hotels to cozy homestays and guesthouses, Phuket offers something for everyone. In this chapter, we will explore the various accommodation choices available, ensuring that you find the perfect place to stay during your visit.

4.1 Luxury Resorts and Hotels

Phuket is renowned for its luxurious resorts and hotels that provide a haven of opulence and comfort. These establishments offer a range of amenities and services designed to cater to the discerning traveler. From stunning ocean views to private pools, spa facilities, and world-class restaurants, luxury resorts in Phuket strive to provide an unforgettable experience. Indulge in the lavishness of these accommodations and let their impeccable service and attention to detail create lasting memories.

4.2 Budget-Friendly Accommodations

For travelers on a tighter budget, Phuket offers numerous budget-friendly accommodation options without compromising on comfort and convenience. Budget hotels and guesthouses provide clean and comfortable rooms at affordable prices. These establishments often offer essential amenities such as air conditioning, Wi-Fi, and friendly staff who can assist with local recommendations and travel arrangements. Stay within your budget while still enjoying a pleasant stay in Phuket.

4.3 Boutique and Unique Stays

If you're seeking a more personalized and distinctive experience, boutique and unique stays in Phuket are the ideal choice. These accommodations often boast charming interiors, artistic décor, and a sense of individuality. Stay in boutique hotels that exude character and style, or opt for boutique resorts tucked away in secluded corners of the island, offering tranquility and exclusivity. Immerse yourself in the charm and intimate ambiance that these accommodations provide.

4.4 Beachfront Villas

Phuket's stunning coastline makes it an ideal destination for those desiring a beachfront getaway. Beachfront villas offer the ultimate in privacy and luxury, allowing you to wake up to breathtaking ocean views and step directly onto the sand. These spacious accommodations often feature private pools, outdoor living areas, and direct access to the beach. Experience the epitome of tropical living by renting a beachfront villa that offers seclusion and a truly immersive beachside experience.

4.5 Homestays and Guesthouses

For travelers seeking an authentic and immersive experience, homestays and guesthouses provide a glimpse into the local way of life. Stay with friendly local hosts who open their homes to guests, offering cozy rooms and warm hospitality. Immerse yourself in the local culture, indulge in homemade traditional meals, and receive firsthand recommendations on the best local attractions and hidden gems. Homestays and guesthouses allow you to forge genuine connections with the locals and create unforgettable memories.

In conclusion, Phuket offers a diverse range of accommodation options to suit every traveler's needs and preferences. Whether you're seeking luxurious indulgence, budget-friendly comfort, unique boutique stays, beachfront villas, or an immersive homestay experience, Phuket has it all. Choose the accommodation option that aligns with your preferences and embark on a memorable stay in the tropical paradise of Phuket.

Chapter 5: Exploring Phuket's Beaches

Phuket, known as the Pearl of the Andaman, is renowned for its stunning beaches that attract travelers from around the world. With crystal-clear turquoise waters, pristine sands, and picturesque surroundings, the beaches of Phuket offer a tropical paradise for beach lovers and sun-seekers. In this chapter, we will explore some of the most popular and breathtaking beaches that Phuket has to offer.

5.1 Patong Beach

Located on the western coast of Phuket, Patong Beach is the island's most vibrant and bustling beach destination. Stretching over three kilometers, this lively beach is a haven for those seeking a mix of sun, sand, and entertainment. Patong Beach offers a plethora of water activities, including jet skiing, parasailing, and banana boat rides. Additionally, the vibrant nightlife of Patong comes alive after sunset, with numerous bars, clubs, and restaurants lining the famous Bangla Road.

5.2 Kata Beach

For a more laid-back and family-friendly beach experience, Kata Beach is an excellent choice. Situated on the southwestern coast, Kata Beach offers a tranquil atmosphere with its soft sands and clear waters. The beach is divided into two sections: Kata Yai (Big Kata) and Kata Noi (Little Kata). Kata Yai is the larger and more popular area, featuring a range of beachfront accommodations, restaurants, and shops. Kata Noi, on the other hand, is quieter and more secluded, perfect for those seeking a peaceful retreat.

5.3 Karon Beach

Just south of Patong Beach lies the long stretch of golden sand known as Karon Beach. With its wide coastline and gentle waves, Karon Beach is a favorite among families and couples. It offers a perfect balance between a lively atmosphere and a relaxed ambiance. Sun loungers, beachside vendors, and water sports activities are available for visitors to enjoy. Karon Beach also provides stunning sunset views, making it an ideal spot for a romantic evening stroll along the shore.

5.4 Surin Beach

Nestled between Kamala and Bang Tao Beaches, Surin Beach is renowned for its pristine beauty and upscale ambiance. Often referred to as "Millionaires Row," this beach attracts visitors with its clear azure waters and fine white sands. Surin Beach offers a more exclusive and sophisticated experience, with luxurious resorts, beach clubs, and high-end dining options. It is a favorite spot for sunbathing, swimming, and indulging in the finer pleasures of beachside living.

5.5 Nai Harn Beach

Located on the southwestern tip of Phuket, Nai Harn Beach is a hidden gem known for its natural beauty and tranquility. Surrounded by lush green hills and framed by clear turquoise waters, Nai Harn Beach offers a picturesque setting. The beach is less crowded compared to other popular beaches on the island, providing a serene environment for relaxation and solitude. Nai Harn Beach is also popular among surfers during the monsoon season when the waves are ideal for riding.

Phuket's beaches offer an array of experiences, from vibrant and lively to serene and secluded. Whether you're seeking adventure, relaxation, or simply a place to soak up the sun, Phuket's beaches have something for everyone. From the vibrant energy of Patong Beach to the peaceful serenity of Nai Harn Beach, each beach has its unique charm that will leave you captivated by the beauty of this tropical paradise.

Chapter 6: Phuket's Cultural and Historical Sites

6.1 Old Phuket Town

Old Phuket Town is a captivating district in Phuket that offers a glimpse into the island's rich history and cultural heritage. This charming area is known for its well-preserved Sino-Portuguese architecture, colorful buildings, and vibrant street art. As you wander through the narrow streets, you'll discover quaint shops, boutique cafes, art galleries, and fascinating museums. The mix of Thai, Chinese, and European influences in architecture reflects Phuket's diverse cultural past. Take a stroll, admire the ornate buildings, and immerse yourself in the atmosphere of this historical gem.

6.2 Big Buddha

Perched atop Nakkerd Hill, the iconic Big Buddha is a must-visit attraction in Phuket. Standing at an impressive height of 45 meters, this grand statue is visible from many parts of the island. The serene ambiance and panoramic views from the site make it a popular spot for both locals and tourists. As you approach the Big Buddha, you'll be struck by its sheer size and the intricate details of the marble construction. Visitors can participate in the daily rituals, such as offering flowers or lighting incense, and experience a sense of peace and spirituality in this remarkable setting.

6.3 Wat Chalong

Deeply rooted in Phuket's religious traditions, Wat Chalong is the largest and most important Buddhist temple on the island. This sacred site attracts devotees who come to pay their respects and seek blessings. The temple's striking architecture, intricate murals, and beautifully adorned pagodas create a visually captivating experience. Visitors can explore the various halls, learn about Buddhist teachings, and witness the ornate decorations that reflect Thai culture and spirituality. Don't miss the opportunity to participate in traditional ceremonies or meditate in the peaceful surroundings of Wat Chalong.

6.4 Phuket Old Town Weekend Market

The Phuket Old Town Weekend Market is a vibrant hub of local culture and culinary delights. Open every Saturday and Sunday, this bustling market showcases an array of street food, traditional snacks, handicrafts, and clothing. As you navigate through the lively stalls, you'll be enticed by the tantalizing aromas and the colorful displays. Indulge in local delicacies, sample freshly prepared Thai dishes, and engage in friendly bargaining with the local vendors. The market's energetic atmosphere, live music, and cultural performances make it an ideal place to experience the authentic flavors and traditions of Phuket.

6.5 Phang Nga Bay

While technically not located in Phuket itself, Phang Nga Bay is an awe-inspiring natural wonder that is easily accessible from the island.

Known for its limestone karsts jutting out of emerald-green waters, this bay offers breathtaking scenery and a tranquil escape from the bustling tourist areas. Visitors can explore the bay on a boat tour, kayak through hidden caves, and marvel at the iconic James Bond Island. The sheer beauty of Phang Nga Bay, with its sheer cliffs and pristine beaches, will leave you in awe and provide an unforgettable experience of nature's majesty.

In Chapter 6, we will delve into Phuket's cultural and historical sites, taking you on a journey through the vibrant streets of Old Phuket Town, the spiritual serenity of the Big Buddha, the reverence of Wat Chalong, the flavors of the Phuket Old Town Weekend Market, and the natural beauty of Phang Nga Bay. Each of these sites offers a unique perspective on Phuket's rich cultural heritage, providing travelers with an opportunity to immerse themselves in the island's traditions, history, and natural wonders. Whether you're a history enthusiast, a spiritual seeker, a food lover, or a nature enthusiast, these cultural and historical sites will undoubtedly leave a lasting impression and enhance your Phuket travel experience.

Chapter 7: Outdoor Activities and Adventures

Phuket, with its stunning natural beauty and diverse landscapes, offers a plethora of outdoor activities and adventures for thrill-seekers and nature enthusiasts alike. In this chapter, we will explore some of the exciting activities that await you in Phuket's great outdoors.

7.1 Snorkeling and Diving

Phuket's crystal-clear waters teem with vibrant marine life, making it a paradise for snorkelers and divers. The region is home to numerous spectacular dive sites, including the famous Similan Islands and Phi Phi Islands. Whether you're a beginner or an experienced diver, there are options available for all skill levels. Immerse yourself in the underwater wonderland, where you can encounter colorful coral reefs, tropical fish, and even majestic sea turtles.

7.2 Island Hopping

Embark on a thrilling island-hopping adventure and discover the hidden gems scattered around Phuket. Hop on a boat and set sail to explore the nearby islands such as Koh Phi Phi, Koh Racha, and Koh Khai. Each island has its unique charm, offering pristine beaches, breathtaking viewpoints, and opportunities for water activities like kayaking, paddle boarding, and snorkeling. Island hopping is a fantastic way to experience the beauty of the Andaman Sea and create unforgettable memories.

7.3 Elephant Sanctuaries

For those seeking a more ethically conscious wildlife experience, Phuket's elephant sanctuaries provide an opportunity to observe and interact with these gentle giants responsibly and sustainably. Visit reputable sanctuaries that prioritize the well-being of elephants and offer educational programs about their conservation. You can feed and bathe the elephants, and even walk alongside them in their natural habitat, fostering a deeper understanding and appreciation for these magnificent creatures.

7.4 Jungle Trekking

Venture into the lush rainforests of Phuket and embark on a thrilling jungle trekking expedition. With various trekking trails available, you can explore the diverse flora and fauna that inhabit the island's interior. Experienced guides will lead you through the dense foliage, pointing out exotic plant species and wildlife along the way. As you hike through the trails, be prepared to encounter hidden waterfalls, natural pools, and breathtaking panoramic views of the island.

7.5 Zip-lining and Canopy Tours

For an adrenaline-pumping adventure, soar through the treetops on a zip-lining and canopy tour. Strap on a harness, glide along steel cables and marvel at the spectacular vistas below. Phuket's zip-lining courses often include suspended bridges, abseiling, and other exciting challenges. Traverse the treetop platforms, surrounded by the sights and sounds of the tropical rainforest. It's an exhilarating experience that offers a unique perspective of Phuket's natural landscapes.

Engaging in outdoor activities and adventures in Phuket allows you to connect with nature, push your boundaries, and create unforgettable memories. From exploring vibrant underwater ecosystems to immersing yourself in the wonders of the jungle, Phuket offers a diverse range of experiences for every adventurer. Remember to choose reputable operators and prioritize sustainable practices to ensure the long-term preservation of these natural treasures. Get ready to embark on an unforgettable journey in Phuket's great outdoors.

Chapter 8: Phuket's Nightlife and Entertainment

Phuket, known for its vibrant nightlife and exhilarating entertainment options, offers a plethora of experiences that cater to all tastes and preferences. Whether you seek lively street parties, cultural performances, or tranquil beachside bars, Phuket's nightlife scene is sure to leave you enthralled. In this chapter, we explore some of the key highlights of Phuket's nightlife and entertainment, including Bangla Road, night markets, cabaret shows, beach clubs and bars, and thrilling Muay Thai boxing matches.

8.1 Bangla Road

Located in the heart of Patong, Bangla Road stands as the epitome of Phuket's nightlife. This bustling street transforms into a vibrant hub of activity as the sun sets. Lined with an array of neon lights, clubs, bars, and entertainment venues, Bangla Road beckons visitors with its lively atmosphere and pulsating energy.

Prepare to immerse yourself in the vibrant beats of music, enjoy the company of fellow partygoers, and indulge in an unforgettable nightlife experience.

8.2 Night Markets

For a more laid-back and cultural evening experience, Phuket's night markets provide a delightful alternative. These markets offer an array of shopping opportunities, local street food, and a chance to immerse yourself in the local culture. Stroll through the bustling aisles, adorned with stalls selling handicrafts, clothing, accessories, and souvenirs. Taste the flavors of Thailand as you sample delectable street food, and witness the lively atmosphere created by locals and tourists alike.

8.3 Cabaret Shows

Phuket's cabaret shows are a unique blend of artistry, talent, and flamboyance. Known for their extravagant costumes and mesmerizing performances, these shows captivate audiences with their glamour and allure. Experience a night of glitz and glamour as talented performers showcase their skills through dance, music, and captivating stage productions. From traditional Thai performances to modern interpretations, Phuket's cabaret shows offer an enchanting evening of entertainment.

8.4 Beach Clubs and Bars

Phuket's pristine beaches serve as the perfect backdrop for its beach clubs and bars. Whether you're seeking a relaxed sunset drink or a night of dancing under the stars, the beach clubs and bars of Phuket cater to a wide range of tastes. Unwind on plush loungers, sip on refreshing cocktails, and soak up the breathtaking ocean views. With a diverse range of venues and atmospheres, you can find the ideal spot to enjoy the pulsating rhythms of music and the vibrant social scene.

8.5 Muay Thai Boxing Matches

For those seeking an adrenaline-fueled evening, witnessing a Muay Thai boxing match is an absolute must. Muay Thai, the national sport of

Thailand, showcases the agility, skill, and power of its fighters. Phuket offers numerous venues where you can experience the excitement and intensity of this ancient martial art. Whether you're a fan of combat sports or simply curious about this unique cultural tradition, attending a Muay Thai boxing match promises an unforgettable night of action and spectacle.

In conclusion, Phuket's nightlife and entertainment scene presents an enticing array of experiences that cater to diverse interests. Whether you choose to party the night away on Bangla Road, explore the vibrant night markets, indulge in captivating cabaret shows, unwind at beach clubs and bars, or witness the raw intensity of Muay Thai boxing matches, Phuket promises to leave you with lasting memories of thrilling evenings and unforgettable entertainment.

Chapter 9: Shopping in Phuket

Phuket is not only known for its stunning beaches and vibrant nightlife but also for its diverse and exciting shopping scene. From modern shopping malls to bustling local markets, the island offers a wide range of retail experiences to suit every taste and budget. In this chapter, we will explore some of the top shopping destinations in Phuket and discover the unique treasures they have to offer.

9.1 Central Festival Phuket

Located in the heart of Phuket Town, Central Festival Phuket is the island's largest and most popular shopping mall. Boasting a vast selection of international and local brands, this multi-level complex caters to all kinds of shoppers. From fashion boutiques and beauty salons to electronics stores and gourmet supermarkets, Central Festival Phuket has it all. After a satisfying shopping spree, visitors can unwind at one of the many restaurants or catch a movie at the state-of-the-art cinema.

9.2 Jungceylon Shopping Mall

Situated in Patong, Jungceylon Shopping Mall is a bustling retail hub that caters to both tourists and locals alike. This expansive mall offers a diverse range of shops, ranging from high-end fashion outlets to souvenir stalls. Visitors can explore well-known international brands, browse through local designer boutiques, or pick up unique souvenirs to commemorate their trip. The mall also houses a wide selection of restaurants, cafes, and entertainment options, making it a popular spot for both shopping and leisure.

9.3 Phuket Weekend Market

For a more authentic and vibrant shopping experience, the Phuket Weekend Market, also known as Naka Market, is a must-visit destination. Located in Phuket Town, this bustling market springs to life every weekend, offering a plethora of goods and local delights. Here, visitors can immerse themselves in a bustling atmosphere filled with colorful stalls selling everything from clothing and accessories to handicrafts and artwork. Exploring the market is a sensory delight, with tantalizing aromas of Thai street food wafting through the air. Be sure to brush up on your bargaining skills, as haggling is a common practice in this lively market.

9.4 Local Handicrafts and Souvenirs

Phuket is known for its rich artistic heritage, and the island is brimming with local artisans and craftsmen who create beautiful handmade products. Whether it's intricate wood carvings, traditional Thai silk, or intricate jewelry, numerous shops, and galleries showcase these unique handicrafts. To truly appreciate the skill and craftsmanship behind these creations, consider visiting places like Ban Boran Textiles or the Old Phuket Town Handicrafts Center. These establishments offer a glimpse into the island's cultural heritage and provide an opportunity to take home one-of-a-kind souvenirs.

9.5 Floating Markets

If you're looking for a truly unique shopping experience, Phuket's floating markets are not to be missed. These vibrant markets are set on waterways, with vendors selling a variety of goods from traditional Thai snacks and fresh produce to handicrafts and clothing. One of the popular floating markets in Phuket is the Bang Rong Floating Market, where visitors can navigate through the lively atmosphere on longtail boats, interact with friendly vendors, and savor local delicacies. The floating markets offer a glimpse into the traditional way of life in Thailand and provide an unforgettable shopping experience.

In conclusion, Phuket offers a diverse and exciting shopping scene that caters to all preferences. Whether you're looking for high-end fashion, local handicrafts, or the thrill of bargaining in a bustling market, the island has it all. From the modern and expansive Central Festival Phuket to the authentic and lively Phuket Weekend Market, shopping enthusiasts are sure to find something to suit their tastes. So, make sure to set aside some time to explore the vibrant shopping destinations and take home unique mementos of your Phuket journey.

Chapter 10: Phuket's Gastronomy

Phuket's culinary scene is a vibrant fusion of flavors, offering a delightful array of dishes that will tantalize your taste buds. From traditional Thai cuisine to fresh seafood delights and local street food, the island caters to every palate. Moreover, Phuket embraces international dining options, ensuring that visitors with diverse culinary preferences can indulge in their favorite cuisines. For those eager to learn the secrets of Thai cooking, Phuket also offers cooking classes and food tours that provide an immersive and educational experience.

10.1 Traditional Thai Cuisine

Thai cuisine is renowned worldwide for its bold and harmonious flavors. In Phuket, you can savor authentic Thai dishes that showcase a balance of sweet, sour, spicy, and savory elements. From aromatic curries like green curry and massaman curry to the tangy som tam (green papaya salad) and flavorful pad Thai, the local restaurants and street food stalls present a rich tapestry of Thai culinary traditions. Make sure to explore the local markets and try regional specialties like moo hong (braised pork belly) and tom yam goong (spicy shrimp soup).

10.2 Seafood Delights

Situated on an island, Phuket boasts an abundance of fresh seafood. The local fishing industry ensures a constant supply of the finest catches from the Andaman Sea. Seafood lovers can relish succulent grilled prawns, crispy fried fish, and mouthwatering seafood platters featuring a variety of shellfish. Raw seafood delicacies like Thai-style ceviche and spicy seafood salads are also popular choices. Be sure to visit the seafood restaurants along the beachfront or venture to the local fishing villages for an authentic seafood dining experience.

10.3 Local Street Food

Exploring the vibrant street food scene in Phuket is a must for any food enthusiast. The bustling night markets and roadside stalls offer an array of delectable treats at affordable prices. From satay skewers and grilled sausages to savory roti and crispy fried chicken, the options are endless. Indulge in local favorites such as pad see ew (stir-fried noodles), khao man gai (chicken rice), and mango sticky rice for a true taste of Phuket's street food culture. Don't forget to sample the refreshing fruit shakes and Thai iced tea to beat the tropical heat.

10.4 International Dining Options

Phuket caters to a diverse international crowd, and its culinary landscape reflects this multicultural influence. You'll find a wide range of international dining options, including Italian, French, Japanese, Indian, and more. Whether you're craving a wood-fired pizza, a perfectly seared steak, or a plate of sushi, Phuket's international restaurants offer an extensive selection of cuisines prepared by skilled chefs. For a romantic evening or a special celebration, the island boasts several elegant fine dining establishments that showcase international flavors with a touch of Thai inspiration.

10.5 Cooking Classes and Food Tours

Immerse yourself in the culinary traditions of Phuket by joining a cooking class or embarking on a food tour. These experiences allow you to learn the art of Thai cooking from local chefs, who will guide you through the preparation of signature dishes using fresh ingredients and traditional techniques. You'll gain valuable insights into the flavors and techniques that make Thai cuisine so special. Food tours take you on a gastronomic journey, introducing you to hidden street food gems and local markets, providing a deeper understanding of Phuket's culinary heritage.

In Chapter 10 of the "Phuket Travel Guide 2023," you'll discover the diverse gastronomic offerings of the island. Whether you choose to savor traditional Thai cuisine, indulge in fresh seafood, explore the vibrant street food scene, or dine at international restaurants, Phuket's culinary delights will leave you with a lasting impression. Additionally, by participating in cooking classes and food tours, you can fully immerse yourself in the rich flavors and cultural heritage of Phuket's gastronomy. Prepare to embark on a culinary adventure that will delight your senses and create unforgettable memories.

Chapter 11: Spa and Wellness in Phuket

Phuket is not only renowned for its stunning beaches and vibrant nightlife but also for its thriving spa and wellness scene. Chapter 11 of the Phuket Travel Guide explores the various opportunities for rejuvenation and relaxation available on the island. From traditional Thai massage to luxurious spa retreats, yoga and meditation centers, detox and wellness programs, and alternative therapies, Phuket offers a range of options to promote wellness of the mind, body, and soul.

11.1 Traditional Thai Massage

At the heart of Phuket's spa and wellness offerings is the traditional Thai massage. This ancient healing art combines acupressure, stretching techniques, and assisted yoga poses to stimulate the body's energy flow and promote overall well-being. Visitors can indulge in authentic Thai massage sessions offered by skilled therapists trained in centuries-old techniques. From beachside massage huts to upscale spa resorts, there are numerous venues across the island where travelers can experience the therapeutic benefits of this age-old practice.

11.2 Luxury Spa Retreats

For those seeking a more indulgent and lavish spa experience, Phuket boasts a wide array of luxury spa retreats. These exquisite establishments offer a range of treatments and therapies in opulent settings, providing a truly pampering experience. From soothing massages and facials to body scrubs and exotic aromatherapy, guests can immerse themselves in a world of relaxation and serenity. These luxury spa retreats often feature stunning ocean views, private treatment villas, and exclusive wellness packages designed to cater to every individual's needs.

11.3 Yoga and Meditation Centers

Phuket's serene natural beauty and tranquil atmosphere make it an ideal destination for yoga and meditation enthusiasts. The island is home to numerous yoga and meditation centers that offer a peaceful sanctuary for practicing these ancient disciplines. Whether you are a beginner or an experienced yogi, you can find a variety of classes, workshops, and retreats tailored to different skill levels and preferences. With experienced instructors and idyllic surroundings, Phuket's yoga and meditation centers provide the perfect setting to unwind, increase mindfulness, and reconnect with oneself.

11.4 Detox and Wellness Programs

Phuket is increasingly recognized as a destination for detox and wellness programs, attracting health-conscious travelers from around the world. These programs typically combine various detoxification methods, such as juice fasting, cleansing diets, and holistic therapies, with fitness activities and educational workshops. Whether you are looking to jump-start a healthier lifestyle, lose weight, or simply rejuvenate your body and mind, Phuket's detox and wellness programs offer comprehensive and personalized approaches to achieving your goals.

11.5 Healing and Alternative Therapies

In addition to traditional spa treatments, Phuket also embraces a range of healing and alternative therapies rooted in ancient Eastern practices. Visitors can explore a multitude of holistic approaches, including Reiki, crystal healing, sound therapy, Ayurveda, and traditional Chinese medicine. These therapies focus on balancing energy, promoting relaxation, and enhancing overall well-being. Many wellness centers and specialized practitioners on the island offer these alternative therapies, providing visitors with unique and transformative experiences.

Chapter 11 of the Phuket Travel Guide introduces readers to the diverse world of spas and wellness in Phuket. Whether you seek traditional Thai massage, luxurious spa retreats, yoga and meditation centers, detox and wellness programs, or alternative therapies, Phuket offers an abundance of opportunities to nurture your body, mind, and spirit. Embrace the serenity of Phuket and embark on a journey of self-care and rejuvenation in this tropical paradise.

Chapter 12: Family-Friendly Activities

Phuket is not only a paradise for beach lovers and adventure enthusiasts but also an ideal destination for families traveling with children. This chapter explores some of the top family-friendly activities in Phuket that offer entertainment, education, and unforgettable experiences for the whole family to enjoy.

12.1 Phuket Aquarium

Located in Cape Panwa, the Phuket Aquarium is a captivating attraction that allows visitors, especially children, to explore the fascinating underwater world. The aquarium showcases an impressive array of marine life, including colorful coral reefs, exotic fish species, and unique sea creatures. With informative exhibits and interactive displays, families can learn about the importance of marine conservation and gain a deeper understanding of the diverse ecosystems that thrive beneath the ocean's surface.

12.2 Phuket Trickeye Museum

For an interactive and mind-bending experience, the Phuket Trickeye Museum in Phuket Town is a must-visit destination. This innovative museum features 3D artworks and optical illusions that trick the eye, creating immersive and playful environments for visitors of all ages. Families can become part of the art as they pose and take pictures with the various exhibits, blending reality and illusion in a fun and imaginative way.

12.3 Splash Jungle Water Park

Located within the Grand West Sands Resort in Mai Khao Beach, Splash Jungle Water Park promises a day of thrilling water adventures for the entire family. With a wide range of exhilarating slides, lazy rivers, and interactive water playgrounds, this water park offers endless entertainment and refreshing fun. Parents can relax on sun loungers while kids splash around in the safe and supervised environment of the park, creating unforgettable memories together.

12.4 Phuket Elephant Sanctuary

For a unique and ethical elephant encounter, the Phuket Elephant Sanctuary provides an unforgettable experience for the whole family. Located in the lush greenery of the Phuket jungle, this sanctuary is dedicated to rescuing and rehabilitating elephants that have been mistreated or exploited. Visitors can observe these majestic creatures in their natural habitat, learn about their behavior, feed them, and even participate in mud baths with the elephants. This experience promotes responsible and sustainable tourism, fostering a deeper appreciation for wildlife conservation.

12.5 Phuket Butterfly Garden and Insect World

Step into a world of enchantment at the Phuket Butterfly Garden and Insect World, where families can discover the beauty and diversity of tropical butterflies and fascinating insects. This botanical garden provides a serene setting filled with vibrant flowers and fluttering butterflies. Visitors can witness the life cycle of butterflies, from caterpillar to chrysalis to graceful flight, and learn about the different species that inhabit the garden. The adjacent insect museum offers a closer look at an extensive collection of insects, including beetles, spiders, and scorpions, providing educational opportunities for curious minds.

In conclusion, Phuket offers a plethora of family-friendly activities that cater to the interests of all ages. From educational experiences at the Phuket Aquarium and Phuket Butterfly Garden and Insect World to interactive and playful adventures at the Phuket Trickeye Museum, families are guaranteed a memorable time together. Additionally, the Splash Jungle Water Park and the Phuket Elephant Sanctuary provide thrilling and ethical experiences that combine entertainment with a focus on environmental conservation. Phuket truly is a destination that offers something special for every member of the family.

Chapter 13: Day Trips from Phuket

Phuket, with its stunning beaches and vibrant culture, serves as an ideal base for exploring the breathtaking natural beauty of the surrounding islands and destinations. In this chapter, we will delve into some of the most popular day trips from Phuket, offering visitors a chance to immerse themselves in the captivating wonders of the Andaman Sea. From pristine beaches and azure waters to dramatic limestone cliffs and enchanting marine life, these destinations promise unforgettable experiences.

13.1 Phi Phi Islands

The Phi Phi Islands, located just a short boat ride from Phuket, have gained international fame for their unparalleled beauty. Comprising two main islands, Phi Phi Don and Phi Phi Leh, this archipelago boasts crystal-clear turquoise waters, powdery white sand beaches, and dramatic cliffs. Visitors can indulge in snorkeling or diving adventures to explore vibrant coral reefs teeming with tropical fish.

Maya Bay, made famous by the movie "The Beach," is a must-visit attraction on Phi Phi Leh. With its stunning scenery, Phi Phi Islands are a true tropical paradise.

13.2 Similan Islands

The Similan Islands, a national marine park consisting of 11 islands, is a paradise for nature enthusiasts and divers. Renowned for their pristine beauty, these islands offer an array of marine life and vibrant coral gardens. Snorkeling and diving in the clear waters allow visitors to witness the splendor of underwater ecosystems, including manta rays, whale sharks, and colorful reef fish. The Similan Islands are a haven for those seeking tranquility and natural wonders.

13.3 Phang Nga Bay

Phang Nga Bay, with its iconic limestone karsts rising dramatically from emerald-green waters, presents a landscape straight out of a postcard. This stunning bay offers a myriad of exploration opportunities, including sea cave kayaking and long-tail boat tours. One of the most famous landmarks in Phang Nga Bay is James Bond Island (Koh Tapu), featured in the James Bond movie "The Man with the Golden Gun." The unique geological formations and serene mangrove forests make Phang Nga Bay an unforgettable destination.

13.4 James Bond Island

Located within Phang Nga Bay, James Bond Island (Koh Tapu) deserves special mention due to its worldwide fame. The distinctive towering limestone rock jutting out of the emerald waters has become an iconic landmark. Visitors can take long-tail boat tours to explore the island, marvel at its natural beauty, and capture memorable photographs. James Bond Island is a must-see attraction for movie enthusiasts and nature lovers alike.

13.5 Krabi and Ao Nang

While not an island, Krabi and its popular beach destination, Ao Nang, are well worth a day trip from Phuket. Just a short distance away, Krabi boasts stunning limestone cliffs, pristine beaches, and lush jungles. Visitors can enjoy a range of activities, including rock climbing, island hopping, and exploring the famous Railay Beach. With its laid-back atmosphere and breathtaking landscapes, Krabi and Ao Nang offer a different perspective on the natural wonders of the Andaman region.

Embarking on day trips from Phuket to these captivating destinations allows travelers to witness the diverse beauty of the Andaman Sea. Whether it's the idyllic Phi Phi Islands, the vibrant marine life of the Similan Islands, the awe-inspiring Phang Nga Bay, the iconic James Bond Island, or the enchanting Krabi and Ao Nang, each destination promises an adventure that will leave visitors with cherished memories of their time in Phuket and its surrounding islands.

Chapter 14: Sustainable Tourism in Phuket

Phuket, renowned for its stunning beaches and vibrant tourism industry, is also committed to promoting sustainable practices and responsible tourism. This chapter explores various initiatives and efforts undertaken in Phuket to foster sustainability and preserve its natural and cultural heritage. By engaging in ecotourism initiatives, promoting responsible diving and snorkeling, supporting community-based tourism projects, implementing wildlife conservation efforts, and encouraging the support of local businesses, Phuket aims to create a harmonious and environmentally friendly tourism destination.

14.1 Ecotourism Initiatives

Phuket is dedicated to developing ecotourism initiatives that prioritize the preservation and conservation of its delicate ecosystems. Through partnerships with local organizations and government bodies, sustainable practices such as waste management, energy conservation, and eco-friendly transportation are being promoted. Visitors can participate in eco-tours that highlight the region's unique flora and fauna, providing educational experiences while minimizing environmental impact.

14.2 Responsible Diving and Snorkeling

Phuket's crystal-clear waters and vibrant marine life make it a popular destination for diving and snorkeling enthusiasts. To protect the marine ecosystem, responsible diving and snorkeling practices are encouraged. Dive operators adhere to strict guidelines to prevent damage to coral reefs and marine habitats, including promoting responsible buoyancy control, avoiding contact with marine life, and using environmentally friendly sunscreen. These efforts ensure that future generations can continue to enjoy the beauty of Phuket's underwater world.

14.3 Community-Based Tourism Projects

Community-based tourism projects have gained momentum in Phuket as a way to empower local communities while preserving their cultural heritage. Visitors can engage in immersive experiences that showcase traditional crafts, cuisine, and customs, directly benefiting residents. By participating in these projects, travelers contribute to the economic development of the communities they visit, fostering sustainable livelihoods and preserving cultural diversity.

14.4 Wildlife Conservation Efforts

Phuket recognizes the importance of protecting its diverse wildlife. Conservation organizations and government initiatives are working diligently to safeguard endangered species and their natural habitats. Efforts include establishing protected areas, promoting responsible wildlife encounters, and implementing educational programs to raise awareness about the importance of conservation. Visitors can actively support these efforts by choosing ethical wildlife tourism experiences and respecting wildlife habitats.

14.5 Supporting Local Businesses

Supporting local businesses is crucial for sustainable tourism in Phuket. By patronizing locally owned accommodations, restaurants, and shops, travelers can contribute directly to the local economy and the well-being of the community. Local businesses often prioritize sustainable practices, source local products, and provide authentic experiences that showcase the unique charm of Phuket. This support fosters a sense of pride within the community and helps maintain the island's cultural integrity.

In conclusion, sustainable tourism in Phuket is a collective effort to protect the environment, preserve cultural heritage, and support local communities. Through ecotourism initiatives, responsible diving and snorkeling practices, community-based tourism projects, wildlife conservation efforts, and supporting local businesses, Phuket strives to ensure a sustainable and responsible travel experience for visitors. By embracing these principles, travelers can contribute to the long-term preservation and enjoyment of Phuket's natural beauty and cultural richness.

Chapter 15: Phuket's Festivals and Events

Phuket is not only known for its stunning beaches and vibrant nightlife but also for its rich cultural heritage and lively festivals. Throughout the year, the island comes alive with vibrant celebrations and events that offer visitors a glimpse into the local traditions and customs. In this chapter, we will explore some of the most prominent festivals and events that take place in Phuket.

15.1 Songkran (Thai New Year)

Songkran, also known as the Thai New Year, is one of the most widely celebrated festivals in Phuket and across Thailand. Taking place annually from April 13th to 15th, Songkran marks the beginning of the traditional Thai calendar. The festival is characterized by joyous water fights and cleansing rituals, symbolizing the washing away of the previous year's misfortunes and welcoming the new year with a fresh start. Locals and tourists alike participate in water battles on the streets, where water guns and buckets are used to drench one another. Traditional ceremonies, such as pouring water over Buddha statues, are also held at temples during this festive period.

15.2 Vegetarian Festival

The Vegetarian Festival, also known as the Nine Emperor Gods Festival, is a significant event for Phuket's Chinese community and attracts visitors from around the world. Held in September or October, the festival spans nine days and is characterized by adherents observing a strict vegetarian diet and performing rituals to purify their bodies and minds. During this period, you will witness processions featuring participants dressed in white, carrying incense, and walking on hot coals. Piercing rituals, where individuals insert various objects through their cheeks and bodies, are also a remarkable and somewhat intense aspect of the festival.

15.3 Loy Krathong

Loy Krathong, often referred to as the Festival of Lights, is a mesmerizing celebration that takes place on the evening of the full moon in November. Participants gather at the water's edge, such as rivers or beaches, to release krathongs, small lotus-shaped rafts made of banana leaves, decorated with flowers, candles, and incense. As the krathongs float away, it is believed that they carry away bad luck and negative energies. The skies are also adorned with lanterns that are released into the air, creating a magical atmosphere. Loy Krathong is a time of reflection, renewal, and gratitude for the abundance of water in Thailand.

15.4 Phuket Old Town Festival

The Phuket Old Town Festival is an annual event that celebrates the unique heritage and culture of Old Phuket Town. Usually held in February, the festival transforms the historic streets into a vibrant carnival of food stalls, traditional performances, art exhibitions, and cultural displays. Visitors can indulge in a wide array of local delicacies, experience traditional music and dance performances, and witness street parades featuring colorful costumes and vibrant floats. The Phuket Old Town Festival provides a fantastic opportunity to immerse oneself in the local heritage and witness the fusion of different cultural influences in Phuket.

15.5 Phuket International Blues Rock Festival

For music enthusiasts visiting Phuket, the Phuket International Blues Rock Festival is an event not to be missed. Held annually, usually in March, this festival attracts talented blues and rock artists from around the world to showcase their skills on stage. The event takes place in a stunning beachfront setting, creating a unique and laid-back atmosphere. Visitors can enjoy live performances, indulge in delicious food and beverages, and soak in the captivating sounds of blues and rock music under the stars. The Phuket International Blues Rock Festival offers a memorable experience for music lovers and contributes to the vibrant cultural scene of the island.

In conclusion, Phuket's festivals and events provide a fascinating window into the island's rich cultural tapestry. Whether it's the exhilarating water fights of Songkran, the intense rituals of the Vegetarian Festival, the enchanting lights of Loy Krathong, the celebration of heritage at the Phuket Old Town Festival, or the soulful music at the Phuket International Blues Rock Festival, each event offers a unique and immersive experience. Attending these festivals allows visitors to connect with the local community, witness centuries-old traditions, and create lasting memories of their time in Phuket.

Chapter 16: Transportation in Phuket

Phuket, with its diverse landscapes and vibrant attractions, offers various transportation options to help visitors navigate the island efficiently. Understanding the transportation system is essential for a smooth and enjoyable travel experience. In this chapter, we will explore the different modes of transportation available in Phuket, ranging from traditional tuk-tuks to modern ride-hailing services. Let's delve into the details of each option:

16.1 Tuk-Tuks and Taxis

Tuk-tuks and taxis are a common sight in Phuket and provide convenient door-to-door transportation. Tuk-tuks are three-wheeled motorized vehicles, while taxis are typically four-wheeled cars. Both options offer a flexible way to explore the island and reach your desired destinations. It's important to negotiate the fare before boarding a tuk-tuk, as they generally do not run on meters. Taxis, on the other hand, operate on a metered system, but it's advisable to confirm the fare with the driver before starting the journey.

16.2 Motorbike Rentals

For those seeking independence and the freedom to explore at their own pace, renting a motorbike is a popular choice in Phuket. Numerous rental shops are scattered throughout the island, allowing visitors to easily obtain a motorbike for a day or longer. However, it is essential to exercise caution and prioritize safety while riding. Always wear a helmet, follow traffic rules, and familiarize yourself with the local driving conditions before embarking on your motorbike adventure.

16.3 Songthaews (Shared Minibuses)

Songthaews, brightly colored shared minibusses, is a cost-effective mode of transportation in Phuket. These vehicles follow specific routes and can be flagged down along the main roads. Songthaews usually operate on fixed fares and are a great option for short to medium distances. They can accommodate multiple passengers, and the driver will drop you off at your requested destination along the route.

16.4 Grab and Uber Services

In recent years, ride-hailing services such as Grab and Uber have gained popularity in Phuket. Using mobile applications, visitors can conveniently book a ride with a private driver. These services provide a reliable and hassle-free transportation experience, with upfront pricing and the convenience of cashless transactions. However, it is worth noting that local regulations and the availability of ride-hailing services may vary, so it's advisable to check the current situation before relying on these options.

16.5 Public Bus System

Phuket's public bus system offers an economical way to traverse the island. The buses operate on designated routes and cover various destinations. The main bus terminal is located in Phuket Town, and from there, buses connect to popular tourist areas, beaches, and other key locations. Public buses are a budget-friendly option, but they may have limited schedules, so it's recommended to check the timetables in advance.

By understanding the transportation options in Phuket, you can choose the most suitable mode of travel based on your preferences, budget, and itinerary. Whether you opt for the convenience of tuk-tuks and taxis, the freedom of motorbike rentals, the affordability of songthaews, the convenience of ride-hailing services, or the cost-effectiveness of the public bus system, Phuket offers a range of choices to cater to your transportation needs. Enjoy exploring the island with ease and comfort as you embark on your Phuket adventure.

Chapter 17: Safety Tips and Travel Advice

When traveling to Phuket, it is essential to prioritize your safety and well-being. This chapter provides valuable information and practical advice to ensure a secure and enjoyable experience throughout your trip. From health and medical services to scam awareness, beach safety, respect for local customs, and emergency contacts, this chapter covers important aspects of staying safe in Phuket.

17.1 Health and Medical Services

Maintaining good health during your trip is crucial for an enjoyable experience in Phuket. Familiarize yourself with the following health and medical services:

Medical Facilities: Phuket is equipped with modern hospitals and medical centers that provide comprehensive healthcare services. Prominent facilities include Bangkok Hospital

Phuket, Siriroj International Hospital, and Mission Hospital Phuket.

Travel Insurance: It is highly recommended to have travel insurance that covers medical emergencies, including hospitalization, evacuation, and repatriation. Ensure your insurance policy is valid in Thailand.

Vaccinations: Before your trip, consult a healthcare professional or travel clinic to determine if any vaccinations are necessary. Common vaccines for Thailand include hepatitis A and B, typhoid, tetanus, and influenza.

Medications: If you require prescription medication, bring an adequate supply for the duration of your stay. It is advisable to carry them in their original packaging, along with a copy of the prescription.

17.2 Scam Awareness

Like any popular tourist destination, Phuket has its share of scams targeting unsuspecting visitors. Stay vigilant and informed to avoid falling victim to scams:

Tuk-Tuk and Taxi Scams: Be cautious when dealing with tuk-tuk drivers and taxis. Always negotiate and agree on the fare before getting in. Insist on using the meter for taxis, and ensure it is functional.

Gem and Jewelry Scams: Exercise caution when purchasing gemstones or jewelry. Stick to reputable shops and request certifications for authenticity. Avoid street vendors offering seemingly lucrative deals.

Tourist Information Scams: Be wary of individuals posing as tourist information agents who offer discounted tours or activities. Book through reputable travel agencies or directly at the official tourism centers.

Jet Ski and Motorbike Rental Scams: Inspect rental vehicles thoroughly before use and document any existing damages. Take photos and make sure the rental agreement clearly states the condition of the vehicle.

17.3 Beach Safety

Phuket's beautiful beaches are major attractions, but it's important to be aware of potential hazards and practice beach safety:

Swim at Designated Areas: Only swim in areas monitored by lifeguards and designated as safe for swimming. Observe warning flags and signs indicating dangerous conditions.

Rip Currents: Be cautious of rip currents, which can be strong and pull swimmers away from the shore. If caught in a rip current, swim parallel to the shore until you escape its pull, then swim back to land.

Sun Protection: Protect yourself from the intense tropical sun by wearing sunscreen with a high SPF, a hat, sunglasses, and lightweight, breathable clothing. Stay hydrated and seek shade during the hottest hours of the day.

Water Activities: Follow safety guidelines and use reputable operators for water activities such as snorkeling, diving, and jet skiing. Ensure proper safety equipment is provided, and never engage in activities under the influence of alcohol.

17.4 Respect for Local Customs

Respecting local customs and traditions is essential to foster positive interactions and demonstrating cultural sensitivity:

Dress Modestly: When visiting temples or religious sites, dress modestly and cover your shoulders and knees. Remove shoes before entering temples and follow any specific rules or guidelines.

Politeness and Courtesy: Thai people value politeness and courteous behavior. Greet locals with a smile and use polite phrases such as "hello" (Sawasdee) and "thank you" (khop khun).

Buddhism Etiquette: When visiting Buddhist temples, observe silence and refrain from touching or photographing religious artifacts without permission. Show reverence and avoid any disrespectful behavior.

Monarchy and National Symbols: Show respect for the Thai monarchy and national symbols. Avoid any form of criticism or disrespectful actions towards the royal family or national symbols.

17.5 Emergency Contacts

In case of emergencies or assistance, it is important to have access to the appropriate contact information:

Police: For emergencies requiring police assistance, dial 191 from any phone.

Tourist Police: The Tourist Police Hotline can be reached at 1155 for non-emergency assistance and general information related to tourism.

Medical Emergency: In case of a medical emergency, dial 1669 for an ambulance or visit the nearest hospital emergency department.

Fire and Rescue: Dial 199 for fire and rescue services in case of emergencies related to fire, accidents, or natural disasters.

Embassy or Consulate: Take note of your country's embassy or consulate contact information in Phuket for any consular assistance or emergencies involving your nationality.

By familiarizing yourself with these safety tips, you can enhance your overall experience in Phuket while ensuring a safe and memorable journey. Remember to exercise caution, stay informed, and prioritize your well-being throughout your travels.

Chapter 18: Learning Basic Thai Phrases

When traveling to a foreign country, it is always helpful to have some knowledge of the local language. In Chapter 18 of the "Phuket Travel Guide 2023," we will delve into learning basic Thai phrases that will enhance your travel experience in Phuket. From greetings and common expressions to essential phrases for various situations, this chapter will equip you with the language skills necessary to navigate and communicate effectively during your stay.

18.1 Greetings and Common Expressions

Mastering basic greetings and common expressions is a great way to break the ice and show respect for the local culture. In this section, you will learn how to say hello, thank you, sorry, and other essential phrases. Understanding the Thai culture's emphasis on politeness will go a long way in creating positive interactions with locals.

18.2 Ordering Food and Drinks

Thai cuisine is renowned for its vibrant flavors and diverse dishes, making dining in Phuket a delightful experience. In this subsection, you will discover useful phrases for ordering food and drinks in restaurants, including how to express dietary preferences, ask for recommendations, and request a bill. With these phrases at your disposal, you can confidently explore the local culinary scene.

18.3 Asking for Directions

Navigating unfamiliar streets and finding your way around Phuket can be challenging, but fear not. In this section, we will provide you with essential phrases to ask for directions, understand responses, and locate key landmarks. Whether you are seeking directions to a beach, a historical site, or a local market, these phrases will assist you in getting to your desired destination.

18.4 Shopping and Bargaining

Phuket is home to bustling markets and vibrant shopping streets, offering a plethora of souvenirs, handicrafts, and clothing. To make the most of your shopping experience, it is essential to learn phrases for bargaining, asking for prices, and expressing your preferences. This section will equip you with the necessary language skills to navigate the vibrant shopping scene and strike a good deal.

18.5 Emergency Phrases

While we hope that your trip to Phuket will be trouble-free, it is always wise to be prepared for unforeseen circumstances. In this final subsection, you will learn vital emergency phrases to handle unexpected situations. Whether it's seeking medical assistance, reporting a lost item, or contacting the authorities, these phrases will help you communicate effectively during emergencies.

By familiarizing yourself with these basic Thai phrases, you will not only enhance your travel experience in Phuket but also foster positive interactions with locals and immerse yourself in the local culture. Remember, even a few simple phrases can make a significant difference in bridging the language gap and creating memorable connections with the people you encounter during your journey.

Chapter 19: Beyond Phuket: Exploring the Region

Phuket is not only a magnificent destination in itself but also serves as a gateway to the stunning natural beauty and cultural wonders of the surrounding region. In this chapter, we will delve into the enchanting destinations that lie beyond Phuket, offering you a chance to expand your horizons and create unforgettable memories. Let's embark on a journey of exploration and discovery as we venture into Krabi Province, Phang Nga Province, the Phi Phi Islands, Khao Lak, and the captivating nearby islands.

19.1 Krabi Province

Located just a short distance from Phuket, Krabi Province is a treasure trove of breathtaking landscapes and outdoor adventures. With its towering limestone cliffs, crystal-clear turquoise waters, and secluded beaches, Krabi presents a paradise for nature enthusiasts and adventure seekers alike.

Discover the world-famous Railay Beach, a haven for rock climbing enthusiasts, or take a long-tail boat ride to the stunning Phi Phi Islands. Explore the mystical Emerald Pool and Hot Springs, or embark on a thrilling jungle trek to the iconic Tiger Cave Temple, offering panoramic views of the surrounding area.

19.2 Phang Nga Province

Nestled along the Andaman Sea, Phang Nga Province entices visitors with its awe-inspiring karst formations, hidden lagoons, and mystical caves. The star attraction here is undoubtedly the renowned Phang Nga Bay, known for its sheer limestone cliffs rising dramatically from the emerald waters. Explore the world-famous James Bond Island, made famous by the movie "The Man with the Golden Gun," or paddle through the serene mangrove forests on a sea kayaking excursion. Don't miss the chance to visit the enchanting Koh Panyee, a floating Muslim fishing village built on stilts.

19.3 Phi Phi Islands

Renowned for their pristine beauty and turquoise waters, the Phi Phi Islands are a must-visit destination for any traveler exploring the region. Dive into the vibrant underwater world as you snorkel or scuba dive amidst colorful coral reefs teeming with marine life. Relax on the picture-perfect beaches of Maya Bay or Bamboo Island, surrounded by towering cliffs and crystal-clear waters. Take a boat tour around the islands, discovering hidden coves, stunning viewpoints, and the famous Viking Cave, home to swiftlet nests used in the production of bird's nest soup.

19.4 Khao Lak

For those seeking tranquility and a slower pace, Khao Lak provides a serene coastal escape. Blessed with unspoiled beaches, lush national parks, and rich biodiversity, this destination offers an idyllic retreat for nature lovers. Visit the Khao Lak Lam Ru National Park, where dense rainforests, cascading waterfalls, and picturesque hiking trails await. Discover the pristine Similan Islands, renowned for their world-class diving spots and vibrant coral reefs.

Immerse yourself in the local culture by visiting the nearby Tsunami Memorial Park and paying homage to the lives lost during the devastating 2004 tsunami.

19.5 Phuket's Nearby Islands

Phuket is surrounded by a collection of captivating islands that are easily accessible and perfect for day trips. Explore the mesmerizing beauty of Coral Island (Koh Hae) as you engage in thrilling water activities such as snorkeling or parasailing. Visit Racha Island (Raya), known for its crystal-clear waters and abundant marine life, offering excellent diving and snorkeling opportunities. Escape to the tranquil and unspoiled Coconut Island (Koh Maphrao), where you can relax on secluded beaches and indulge in rejuvenating spa treatments.

As you venture beyond Phuket, you will be rewarded with a diverse array of natural wonders, cultural experiences, and captivating landscapes. Each destination has its unique charm, waiting to be explored and cherished. So, set forth on your journey and unlock the hidden gems of Krabi Province, Phang Nga Province, the Phi Phi Islands, Khao Lak, and Phuket's nearby islands. Your adventure into the region promises to be an extraordinary and enriching experience, leaving you with cherished memories that will last a lifetime.

Chapter 20: Conclusion and Farewell to Phuket

As your journey in Phuket comes to a close, it's time to reflect on the experiences you've had, cherish the memories you've made, and bid farewell to this enchanting destination. In this final chapter, we explore various aspects that will help you conclude your Phuket adventure in a meaningful way.

20.1 Reflections on Your Phuket Journey

Take a moment to pause and reflect on the incredible journey you embarked upon in Phuket. Consider the breathtaking beaches you lounged on, the vibrant markets you explored, and the cultural landmarks you encountered. Ponder the encounters with the warm-hearted locals and the flavors of the delectable Thai cuisine. Allow yourself to fully immerse in the memories created during your time in Phuket and appreciate the personal growth and discoveries that unfolded throughout your journey.

20.2 Memories and Souvenirs

Memories are the treasures we carry with us long after we've left a destination. Remember to capture the essence of Phuket by collecting souvenirs that will serve as tangible reminders of your time in this tropical paradise. Whether it's a handcrafted piece of jewelry, a traditional Thai artwork, or a locally produced handicraft, choose items that hold sentimental value and evoke the unique spirit of Phuket. These souvenirs will not only decorate your home but also serve as conversation starters, allowing you to share your experiences with friends and family.

20.3 Planning Your Next Visit

Although your current journey in Phuket is coming to an end, let it be the stepping stone to future adventures. Phuket offers a multitude of attractions and experiences, so consider planning a return visit to explore further. Make a list of the places you didn't get a chance to visit, the activities you didn't have time for, and the hidden gems you've heard about but couldn't explore this time. With each visit, you'll uncover new facets of Phuket's beauty and find yourself captivated by its allure once again.

20.4 Saying Goodbye to Phuket

Saying goodbye to Phuket can be bittersweet, as the memories and experiences you've had here will forever hold a special place in your heart. Take a moment to bid farewell to the stunning beaches, the vibrant streets, and the welcoming locals who made your time in Phuket unforgettable. Embrace the serenity of the island one last time, savoring the tranquil moments and the gentle ocean breeze. Express gratitude for the opportunity to have experienced Phuket's wonders and carry that gratitude with you as you continue your journey in life.

20.5 Acknowledgments and Credits

A project of this magnitude requires the collaboration and expertise of many individuals. We extend our heartfelt thanks and appreciation to the people who contributed to the creation of this Phuket Travel Guide. Our gratitude goes to the local experts, travel enthusiasts, writers, photographers, editors, and researchers who dedicated their time and passion to curating the valuable information contained within this book. Their collective efforts have helped shape this guide into a comprehensive resource for travelers seeking an exceptional experience in Phuket.

Additionally, we would like to express our gratitude to the local authorities, tourism organizations, and businesses in Phuket who have been instrumental in providing the necessary support and information. Their commitment to promoting Phuket as a world-class travel destination has played a significant role in making this guide possible.

Finally, we extend our heartfelt thanks to you, the reader, for choosing this guide as your companion in exploring Phuket. We hope it has enriched your travel experience and inspired you to create lasting memories in this tropical paradise. Safe travels and until we meet again, farewell to Phuket.

Printed in Great Britain
by Amazon